CELEBRATE

COMMUNION

COLLEEN BRITTON

ACKNOWLEDGEMENT

I would like to thank Leo Nelson and the congregation of the Vacaville Church of the New Covenant in Vacaville, California, for their support and encouragement, the chidren of the church for their enthusiasm, Robert and Linda Davidson of Educational Ministries, Inc.. for their assistance and faith in my work, and Jack, Troy, and Shelly for their patience and understanding. A special thanks to REA.

DEDICATED TO

God's kids, young and old

CELEBRATE COMMUNION
by Colleen Britton

Copyright © 1984
EDUCATIONAL MINISTRIES, INC.

Scripture quotations unless otherwise noted are from the **Revised Standard Version of the Bible,** copyright © 1946, 1952, and 1971 by the Division of Christian Education of the National Council of Churches.

ISBN 0-940754-26-6

EDUCATIONAL MINISTRIES, INC.
165 Plaza Drive
Prescott, AZ 86303-5549

TABLE OF CONTENTS

PREFACE

Most of us were raised in a tradition which did not allow children to participate in the Lord's Supper until, at the age of discretion, they became "communicant members" of the church. In recent years we find that children are often invited to partake in the Lord's Supper from early childhood. This is both a great blessing and a tremendous responsibility.

Our children make a real contribution to the life and vitality of the church. Their presence makes our worship a joyful, spontaneous experience. Through their interaction with the entire congregation we all learn more about giving, sharing, caring and loving one another. By welcoming them at the Lord's Supper, we are saying, "Yes, they do belong and are an important part of the church fellowship."

Time and time again Jesus demonstrated his special love for children. *"Of such,"* he said, *"are the Kingdom of God,"* and *"He took them in his arms and blessed them."* The Bible tells us that the promise of life in Christ is given *"to you and TO YOUR CHILDREN."*

Christ does not require a full knowledge and understanding of the meaning and symbolism surrounding the Lord's Supper before we can participate. Instead, he invites all to come to him with the simple trust of children and with the expectation that through participation in the Supper, within the fellowship of the church, the Holy Spirit will move in each of our lives and join us in "Holy Communion".

As adults we approach every Lord's Supper with this expectation. Each Communion Sunday, through scripture, sermon, prayer and song, we bring new thoughts which enlarge our understanding of Sacrament. Herein lies the challenge to Christian Education. We need to provide our children with this same sort of food for the soul so that their understanding of God's love comes alive through the Sacrament.

In our church school we meet this challenge by providing the children with a continuing study of the Lord's Supper. Each time we as a church celebrate Communion, the children leave the sanctuary for a brief time during the sermon and have a special lesson of their own related to the Lord's Supper. They then return to the sanctuary and participate with the entire congregation in the celebration of the Sacrament.

By immediately reinforcing the Communion lesson with participation in the Sacrament, our children, like ourselves, build an understanding of the Lord's Supper as the highest privilege in Christian worship. The feelings of fellowship and reverence that are shared by the congregation during the Communion service also help a great deal to enrich the children's understanding and appreciation of the Sacrament.

A brief outline of our Communion study and suggestions for related activities at home were distributed to parents so they could reinforce and enlarge upon each lesson. This kind of intergenerational sharing helped us all to experience the Lord's Supper more completely.

As our Communion studies progressed, we began planning Communion services which involved the entire congregation in various growing, learning, and sharing activites. Our efforts not only resulted in our children learning more about Communion, but we discovered that the whole congregation had been blessed with a richer Communion experience.

The Communion lessons in this series are planned to be presented to broadly graded classes in 15-20 minute sessions. They can be used during Sunday morning services, as learning center activities during a retreat, family night, vacation church school, or as part of a special Lenten study about Communion. Most are especially well suited for intergenerational experiences. They are a valuable supplemental resource for any church school curriculum.

Also included in this series are outlines for several innovative Communion services and Communion related learning center activities which will enrich your entire congregation's understanding of the Lord's Supper.

SECTION 1

COMMUNION LESSON PLANS

"Do This In Remembrance Of Me"

MAIN IDEA: Christ gave us the Lord's Supper to help us remember him, the greatness of God's love and Christ giving his life for us.

SCRIPTURE: Luke 22:19 *"...This do in remembrance of me."* (KVJ)

LEARNING ACTIVITIES:

• Bring in various "TO DO" lists such as grocery lists, errands to run, bills to pay etc. Talk about why people make lists. (to help them remember)

• Discuss other ways we have of remembering things, tieing string around a finger, etc.

• Have students look up and read Luke 22:19.

• Discuss, "What is it that Jesus wants us to remember? What does he tell us to do to help us remember? How does breaking bread and drinking wine help us remember all that Jesus did for us?"

• Have students each tie a string around a finger to remind them about the meaning of the Lord's Supper. Tell them to take the string off only after they have explained at least one reason for celebrating Communion to someone else—parents or friends. Telling is still another way to help us remember.

• Close with prayer.

MATERIALS:

• Bible

• To Do list

• String and scissors

"The Communion Of Saints"

MAIN IDEA: The observance of Worldwide Communion on the first Sunday of October provides an excellent opportunity to emphasize the common bond we share through Christ, with Christians around the world.

SCRIPTURE: 1 Corr. 12:26 Unity in diversity, many members of one body.

LEARNING ACTIVITIES:

• Have students read the Bible verses 1 Corrinthians.

• Briefly discuss differences in customs, traditions, etc. of various denominations and reinforce the words of Paul, that we are one in Christ. This "oneness" we celebrate together on Worldwide Communion Sunday. We are not alone in our worship of Christ, we share it with believers worldwide.

• Have students make a bulletin board to express the main idea of the lesson. The caption might read, "We Are One Through Christ".

• Illustrations which show people at worship in various settings, churches around the world, close-ups of people from other lands, and pictures of the Communion elements or the Last Supper will help tell the story visually. Pictures can be arranged around a large world map.

• The finished board may be shared with the congregation following the service or as part of it.

• Close with prayer.

MATERIALS:

• Bibles

• Pictures

• Bulletin board and pins

• Scissors

• Map

• Felt pen, paper

LESSON 3

"Give Thanks"

MAIN IDEAS: Come to the Lord's Supper with thanksgiving, being thankful for all God has given us—especially for Christ.

Pause before EVERY meal and make it a special time to give thanks to God.

SCRIPTURE: Luke 22:19 *"He took bread and gave thanks..."*

LEARNING ACTIVITIES:

• Have students look up and read the Bible verse.

• Discuss the circumstances surrounding the Last Supper. Jesus knew he would soon be betrayed, arrested and crucified, yet he still gave thanks to God. What was he thankful for?

• Show a print of the famous painting "Grace", which depicts an old man alone at a table with a small loaf of bread. What do you suppose this man is thankful for? Many people around the world live in poverty, yet they praise God and give Him thanks. Why?

• Discuss our many blessings and the blessing of Christ's presence with us. As we come to the Communion table let us remember all that God has given us and give thanks, especially for His Son who has shown us the greatness of God's love, and has promised to be with us always.

• Ask students to share a special grace they may say at home.

• Encourage the youth to volunteer to say grace at the next family meal and express their thankfulness.

MATERIALS:

• Bible   • Picture of "Grace"

• Pictures of people in poverty yet worshiping and happy

NOTE: When we presented this lesson, one of our youth was from a Scandanavian family which said grace in Dutch. He taught the class a new grace. Encourage the youth to share their family traditions. It helps bring students closer together and learn the meaning of Christian fellowship.

"Ring Christmas Bells"

MAIN IDEA: Communion is a celebration of Christ coming into our world and his continued presence with us.

SCRIPTURE: Luke 2:10-11 "*.. I bring you good news of a great joy which will come to all people...*"

LEARNING ACTIVITIES:

• Have the youth read the Christmas story in Luke 2:10-18. Discuss the angels' message and the shepherds' response.

• Discuss what we celebrate at Christmas and various ways we celebrate. Discuss symbols used at Christmas that remind us of Jesus, e.g., the evergreen tree is a reminder of God's eternal love; angels and stars, reminders of his birth.

• Christmas bells make us happy and help us rejoice at the news of Christ's coming. A communion cup is a reminder of Christ's giving himself freely for us, and a reminder of his presence with us.

• Have the youth make a Christmas bell ornament or corsage from plastic Communion cups as a reminder of his coming into the world, his life, and his continued presence with us. (See Learning Activities for instructions.)

• You may want to make enough corsages to give to the congregation during the Communion service that follows. Some could be made ahead of time.

• The corsages are also welcomed gifts at convalescent homes and hospitals.

• Close with prayer.

MATERIALS:

• Bibles

• Communion cups with small hole in bottom

• Sprig of holly or other greenery

• Glitter, glue

• Wire

• Safety pins

LESSON 5

"New Beginnings"

MAIN IDEA: Communion is a reminder that all things are made new through Christ.

SCRIPTURE: 2 Cor. 5:17-18 *"We are new creatures in Christ."*

LEARNING ACTIVITIES:

• Show pictures of infants, baby animals, early morning scenes, a budding flower to stimulate discussion about the wonder and excitement of new beginnings.

• Pictures of Zacchaeus, Matthew, Mary Magdalene and others can lead the discussion into how Jesus changed the lives of these people, gave them a new beginning, and how he continues to bring hope and joy into our lives.

• Share a magazine or newspaper article about someone whose life has been changed by Christ.

• Compare last year's appointment calendar to a new one with no notations on it. Pass out new calendars to the students. These can serve as a reminder that the New Year is indeed ahead of them and its opportunities through Christ are unlimited.

• Students may want to decorate the calendar cover with a communion symbol e.g., chalice, grapes, bread, wheat, cross, fish.

• Emphasize that the celebration of the Communion is a celebration of the new life and opportunities that come through Jesus Christ.

• Close with prayer.

MATERIALS:

• Bibles

• Small calendars for each student

• Pictures of new life, Zacchaeus, Matthew, Mary Magdalene

• Calendars, new and old

• Materials to decorate calendar covers

"Be My Valentine"

MAIN IDEA: Communion is an expression of God's love for us, His willingness to give Himself freely. It is also an expression of love for God and one another.

SCRIPTURE: John 3:16 *"God so loved the world that He gave His only Son..."* Luke 10:25-28 *"...you shall love the Lord your God with all your heart, mind, and soul..."* John 13:34-35 *"...love one another as I have loved you..."* 1 John 4:7-8 *"...love one another, for God is Love..."*

LEARNING ACTIVITIES:

• Discuss Valentine's Day: what it means to the youth, various ways we show that we love and care for someone, etc.

• Introduce the Bible verses as showing us something about God's love for us, our love for Him and for one another.

• Divide the verses between several young people or groups and have them read and tell what the verses mean in their own words.

• Have the youth recall the Communion service and relate it to the verses about love. Of what does the Communion remind us about God's love for us? About our love for Christ and one another? Through the Communion we are truly bound together in love.

• Have the young people work individually or in groups as they write an acrostic for the word Valentine's Day. The acrostic should reflect what they have learned about God's love, Christ's love, our love for God, Christ and one another. (See Learning Activities for sample acrostic.)

• Read several acrostics aloud, and close with prayer.

MATERIALS:

• Bibles

• Pencils, paper

"The New Covenant"

MAIN IDEA: Through the Lord's Supper we have the New Covenant, the new promise of God's love, which is new life in Christ.

SCRIPTURE: Luke 22:20 *"...this cup is the new covenant..."*

LEARNING ACTIVITIES:

• Have the youth look up the definitions of covenant, promise, and testament. Discuss the meanings of these words. In what ways are they alike and different?

• Examine the title pages of several different Bibles. You will notice that occasionally the New Testament is called the New Covenant. What does that tell us about people and their relationship to God in the Old and New Testament? What was the "Old Covenant"?

• Cut out a piece of paper in the shape of a chalice. Have the young people write what the New Covenant means to them. Tell them to keep the paper with them and read it silently to themselves before they drink of the Communion cup. They may also want to share their ideas with the person sitting next to them.

• Close with prayer.

MATERIALS:

• Bibles

• Dictionaries

• Construction paper chalices

• Pencils

"Resurrection Symbols"

NOTE: This lesson can be repeated using different resurrection symbols and activities each time. It is especially appropriate for use during Lent or Easter.

MAIN IDEA: Communion is a celebration of our renewed fellowship with Christ.

SCRIPTURE: Luke 24:34 *"The Lord has risen indeed..."*

LEARNING ACTIVITIES:

• Write the word "Resurrection" on the board and draw from students their understanding of the word.

• Have students read different accounts of the resurrection story and retell them in their own words:

• Matthew 28:1-10, Mark 16:1-15, Luke 24:13-43, John 21:1-14. Discuss some of the similarities and differences between the stories.

• Jesus' victory over death and his RENEWED FELLOWSHIP with his disciples is RESURRECTION, and it is certainly cause for celebration. WE ARE INCLUDED IN THIS FELLOWSHIP and in this RESURRECTION CELEBRATION. It's not just something that happened 2,000 years ago. Christ is present with us today. We experience his presence through Communion.

• Show examples of resurrection symbols and discuss why each has become a reminder of the resurrection.

• Lily (from dead-looking bulb to flower.)

• Pomegranate (bursting forth from its hard shell like Christ bursting forth from the tomb.)

• Butterfly (changes from caterpillar to a seemingly dead chrysalis, and finally emerges as a beautiful butterfly.)

- Peacock (each time it loses one of its plooms, a more beautiful one replaces it)

- Easter egg (new life contained in hard shell; the shell represents the stone covering Christ's tomb)

• Communion is a celebration of our renewed fellowship with Christ.

• Close with prayer

NOTE: Other activities for this session might include:

- Eating pomegranates

- Making paper butterflies (See Learning Activities)

- Decorating eggs (See Learning Activities)

- Make or plant lilies

MATERIALS:

• Bibles

• Pictures or samples of resurrection symbols: egg, pomegranate, butterfly, lily, peacock.

• YOUNG READER'S BOOK OF CHRISTIAN SYMBOLISM. Michael Daves, Abington Press. N.Y., 1967.

"You're Invited"

MAIN IDEAS: 1. We have been invited to share fellowship with God through Jesus Christ.

2. God, like the master, is eager to share His love with all who accept His invitation.

3. The bread and wine remind us that Christ is present with us as host of the Lord's Supper.

SCRIPTURE: Luke 14:15-24 *"...Come, for all is now ready...urge everyone you find to come, so that the house will be full."*

LEARNING ACTIVITIES:

• Have the youth read the Bible verses, and discuss the story and its symbolism.

• On a chalk board or paper have students make a list of the characters in the parable and who they represent.

• Compare students' ideas of a banquet to their ideas about the Kingdom of God.

• Relate the banquet invitation to Christ's invitation to the Communion and his promise to be with us always.

• Give invitations to Communion to all the students.

MATERIALS:

• Bibles

• Invitations

• Chalk board, chalk or paper and felt pens

LESSON 10

"Making Music"

MAIN IDEA: The richness of God's love is like playing a musical instrument. Study and practice brings understanding and appreciation: sharing it brings joy.

SCRIPTURE: John 3:16 *"God so loved the world, that he gave his only son, that whoever believes in him should not perish but have eternal life."*

LEARNING ACTIVITIES:

• Have the youth read the Bible verse, and discuss how Jesus showed us the greatness of God's love throughout his life and by freely giving himself for us on the cross.

• Find out which of the youth play musical instruments, and introduce the story "The Music Lesson". As you read or retell the story, encourage students to recall their own similar experiences. Share experiences after the story.

• You may want to show your own musical instrument to the class and play a tune.

• Through discussion relate the gift of music to the gift of God's love:

   • It is given freely to all.

   • We can ignore or misuse it, or through Bible study, prayer. Christian fellowship, and with the gift of the Holy Spirit, we can find ETERNAL LIFE AND JOY in His love.

• Communion is a very special way of sharing God's love with other Christians.

   • Through the bread and wine we are joined with Christ in a way that we don't fully understand, but we gratefully accept.

   • By studying about communion in class and Bible studies, asking questions, and by learning as they participate with the rest of the congregation, students deepen their understanding of the sacrament.

- Encourage the youth to continue striving for a fuller understanding of God's love as shown to us through Christ as they partake in the Communion.

- Close with prayer.

MATERIALS:

- Bibles   • Story "The Music Lesson"

THE MUSIC LESSON

"Listen to this, Mom. I can play the whole song now!" With great deliberation, Troy cautiously plucked each string of his new guitar. His steady concentrated gaze turned into a wide grin when he strummed the final chord. As I applauded his efforts, my mind flashed back to a Christmas morning long ago when I had my first music lesson.

At the bottom of our stockings, my brother Bill and I had both found small harmonicas. Delighted and surprised we instantly began to "play", blowing and drawing, moving quickly from one end of the mouthpiece to the other. The noise was too much, and before long, Dad came into the room with his harmonica and a music book.

"Want to learn how to play the right way? Come over here and I'll show you how."

He played several songs, and we sat in awe as he explained and demonstrated each step. There was so much to be learned; how to hold it, how to place your tongue over the holes so that a single tone could be played, how to move your hands to create more mellow sounds. The list went on and on, and then there was reading music. It was a whole new language, every note having a different name and different timing. It was overwhelming!

The learning process was slow indeed. He worked with us every day, and often in the evenings we'd gather around the music stand to practice playing scales and simple songs.

I remember the satisfaction we felt when finally, the three of us played harmony with one another. Later, Bill and I both learned to play other instruments and shared our music with friends at school and at home. The joy of music has been an important part of our family gatherings ever since.

We received much more than a harmonica that year. We received the gift of music, which has to be studied to be mastered and appreciated, and shared to be fully enjoyed.

The gift of God's Love is like that. It is given freely to all of us, even before we ask. We can ignore and misuse it, or we can let God our Father teach us to live in His Love through His Word and His Holy Spirit. Living in His love, we find Life and Joy, which like music, must be shared with others to be complete.

"God's Love Can Be Seen Everywhere"

MAIN IDEA: The world is full of signs and symbols of God's love — Communion is one of them.

SCRIPTURE: Psalm 148

LEARNING ACTIVITIES:

• Have the youth read Psalm 148 in unison and discuss its main theme.

• Examine one or two hymns as time permits: "This Is My Father's World" and "For the Beauty of the Earth". Sing them, discuss the meaning of the words. If possible, show slides or pictures which can illustrate each verse or phrase.

• Help the youth become more aware of the wonder of God's creation and how the beauty of that creation is a reminder of His Love.

• Encourage them to describe scenes of great beauty they have seen: sunsets, mountains, oceans, etc.

• Show pictures of Communion. Emphasize that Communion is another important symbol of God's love because it reminds us of Jesus, whom God sent and who loves us and is always present with us.

• Close with prayer.

MATERIALS:

• Bibles

• Hymnals or word sheets

• Slides or photos to illustrate hymn

• Photos or other symbols of Communion

"Celebrating Communion: Christ's Presence With Us"

MAIN IDEA: Communion is celebrating Christ's presence with us.

SCRIPTURE: Luke 22:19 *"...Do this in REMBRANCE of Me."* Matthew 28:20 *"...I am with you always..."*

LEARNING ACTIVITIES:

• Examine pictures of various celebrations: birthday party, wedding, adult and child happy, church service. Discuss what is happening in each picture. What are they celebrating? Why? What is a celebration? What makes something special enough to celebrate?

• Look up the meaning of the word celebration in the dictionary.

• Worship is a special kind of celebration when we gather together to give thanks and praise God for all the blessings we have received through His son, Jesus.

• Examine a weekly church bulletin. How many different ways do we worship God? On the chalk board or large paper make a list of what happens during a worship service: singing, prayer, scripture reading, sermon, offering, Communion, etc.

• Examine pictures of Jesus with disciples after the resurrection. What is happening? Why are they celebrating? How do we celebrate Christ's presence with us? (Communion)

• Have the youth read the Bible verse. The word remembrance means more than just remember, it implies that as we remember, he will be present with us, ALWAYS! The real reason for celebrating hasn't changed in all these years. He is with us indeed! Alleluia!

• Close with prayer.

MATERIALS:

• Bibles   • Church bulletins

• Pictures of celebrations

"Bread Of Life"

This is a lesson which has many possible main ideas and scripture verses that apply to the learning activities. You may choose those most appropriate for your group or decide to repeat the lesson using different main ideas and activities.

MAIN IDEA AND SCRIPTURE POSSIBILITIES:

1. Main Idea: We need more than physical nourishment to live the full lives that God intended for each of us.

Scripture: Matthew 4:4 *"Man shall not live by bread alone."*

2. Main Idea: Just as bread provides nourishment for our physical bodies, so Jesus is the sustaining nourishment for eternal life.

Scripture: John 6:22-59 *"I am the bread of Life"* and v. 63 *"It is the Spirit that gives life..."*

3. Main Idea: We trust God to meet our needs.

Scripture: Matthew 6:11 *"Give us this day our daily bread..."*

4. Main Idea: The bread served during Communion is of Christ freely giving himself for us.

Scripture: Luke 22:19 *"...This is my body which is given for you..."*

5. Main Idea: Unleavened bread is a reminder of the Passover and the Exodus.

Scripture: Exodus 12:15, Exodus 13:6-8

BACKGROUND:

Bread was indeed the staff of life for the people of Jesus' day. It was often given as a gift and was symbolic of life itself. Bread was never cut with a knife, but rather out of reverence for life, it was broken in the hands.

Jesus knew that bread provided persons with the necessary nourishment for their physical bodies. He also knew that our spiritual bodies need nourishment too. Jesus is the nourishment that we need for our souls. When he talked about those who "...*eat my flesh and drink my blood...*" as never hungering or thirsting again, John 6:56, he was saying that those who partake of life in and through him will find fulfillment. They will have no need to seek something in life more satisfying.

LEARNING ACTIVITIES:

• Discuss the importance of bread as food both in biblical times and today.

• Have the youth read selected Bible verses and discuss their meaning.

• Have the youth form dough into small flat patties on their wrists, bake in a clay oven and eat with butter and honey as you continue discussion.

• Bake enough small cakes to use in the Communion service.

• Have the youth carry two plates of their bread into the sanctuary as Communion is about to be served.

MATERIALS:

• Bread dough: mix together in large bowl; 3 cups Bisquick, 1 cup milk.

• Vegetable oil (a couple drops rubbed on hands and wrists will keep dough from sticking to skin)

• Charcoal, starter, matches

• Large flat metal pan, Bar-BQ bowl or hollowed area in dirt in which to place hot coals.

• Large clay catch pot — turn upside down and cook on the bottom. See figure 1.

• 3 large stones or bricks to keep catch pot off the ground and allow air to reach the coals.

• Honey, butter, knife

• Water to extinguish the coals

• Towel to wipe hands, hot pad

Figure 1

"Symbols of Communion And The New Covenant"

MAIN IDEA: Symbols are reminders. The goal of this lesson is to familiarize students with the meaning of various symbols associated with Christ and the Communion.

SYMBOLS AND THEIR MEANING:

MONOGRAMS FOR CHRIST:

XP — The Chi Rho symbol, an ancient monogram of Christ, appears often on altars, book marks, antependia, and stoles. The most usual form consists of the P within the X. The monogram has been in Christian use for at least 1600 years. Constantine the Great had the monogram of Christ placed on the shields of his soldiers. The symbol is derived from the first two letters of the Greek word XPICTOC (pronounced Christos). The letters abbreviate the name of Christ.

IHS — These letters stand for the first three letters of the Greek word for Jesus (IXEOYE). When knowledge of Greek declined, the Latin letter S was substituted for the Greek letter sigma.

INRI — This is a reminder of the inscription which Pilate had placed on the cross above Jesus' head. It stands for the Latin inscription, IESUS NAZARENUS REX IUDAEORUM. This means, Jesus of Nazareth, King of the Jews.

COMMUNION SYMBOLS:

THE CHALICE — The original cup used by Jesus at the Last Supper has been lost, but a sometimes richly decorated chalice has become a reminder of that first meal. For hygienic reasons, many congregations have replaced the chalice with small communion cups, but it remains a beautiful reminder of the cup which Christ took and blessed at the Last Supper.

CLUSTER OF GRAPES — The grapes represent the Holy Communion because wine, or grape juice which is used in the sacrament is made from grapes. We are reminded of Jesus' words as he gave the wine to his disciples, *"This is my blood of the new covenant, which is poured out for many."*

BREAD — The loaf of bread is a symbol of Christ, the bread of life. Often small pieces are used during the Communion service. When a single loaf of bread is used, it reminds us of the oneness we have in Christ. (1 Corinthians 10:17)

WHEAT — Since bread is made from wheat, a sheaf of wheat is also a familiar symbol of the Lord's Supper. It continues to remind us that those who come to him shall not hunger, and those who believe in him shall never thrist, (John 6:35).

LEARNING ACTIVITIES:

• Discuss symbols, what they are and why we use them. Ask the youth for examples of familiar symbols e.g., stop lights, wedding ring, monograms.

• Examine monogrammed towels, luggage, stationery, jewelry, etc. Discuss the monogram as a sign of ownership.

• Let the young people combine their initials to form monograms on paper or a chalkboard.

• Introduce several monograms of Jesus Christ and discuss how they are used to show that we are his: XP—Chi Rho, IHS—IHEOYE, INRI—Iesus Nazarenus Rex Iudaeorum.

• Show examples of other Communion symbols and discuss their meaning: chalice, grapes, bread, sheat of wheat.

• Have the youth draw, paint or color their favorite monogram and Communion symbol.

• Encourage the youth to look for the symbols in the sanctuary when they return for Communion.

• Close with prayer.

MATERIALS:

• Samples of monograms

• Examples of Communion symbols

• Paper, crayons, pencils

• Church catalogs have many good illustrations of symbols and monograms used in the church.

"The Communion Seal"

MAIN IDEA: Understanding the phrase, *"SEALED with My blood."*

SCRIPTURE: Matthew 26:27-28 *"...Each one drink from it, for this is my blood, sealing the New Covenant..."* **L.B.**

LEARNING ACTIVITIES:

• Discuss ways to seal an agreement, making it official and binding. e.g., handshake, kiss. The Indians used to sometimes seal an agreement with blood.

• Examine official state seals or other similar documents so students can see what an "official seal" looks like today. Personal letters are sometimes sealed with wax seals. These were used quite frequently in Biblical times to guarantee that an article was genuine and had not been previously opened.

• Discuss how covenants, agreements were sealed in Old Testament times. (Exodus 24:1-8) Moses sealed the covenant between God and the Israelites by sprinkling the blood of animals over the altar and the people.

• Have the young people read the verse from Matthew. The promise of God's love to all is sealed with Christ's blood.

• The cross and Communion are reminders of Christ's life freely given for us as a guarantee to "seal" the promise of God's love.

• Distribute small gold cross seals as a reminder of the lesson.

• Close with prayer.

MATERIALS:

• Bibles

• Examples of seals (contact you state legislator, a notary public, church records, stationery store, etc.)

• Gold cross seals

"Visual Interpretations Of The Lord's Supper"

MAIN IDEA: Have the young people experience the Last Supper through the eyes of various famous artists, and then interpret the event through their own art work.

SCRIPTURE: Luke 22:7-30 The Last Supper

LEARNING ACTIVITIES:

• Have the youth read the account of the Lord's Supper in one or more Gospels. Encourage them to visualize the scene as the verses are read and share what they "see" in their mind.

• The life of Christ has without a doubt inspired some of the greatest art in our history. The Lord's Supper has been recorded by many artists from various countries across the centuries.

• Show slides and flat pictures of as many different interpretations of the Last Supper as possible. Encourage students to look for the number of people shown in the picture, their placement at the table, setting of the room, symbols and other points of interest.

• Have the youth draw, paint, etc. their interpretation of the Last Supper. Encourage them to focus on one part of the meal they feel is most important, who was there, the setting of the room etc.

• Encourage them to finish their drawings at home and return them next week. An exhibit of student's work would be a meaningful accent to the sanctuary during the next Communion service.

• Close with prayer.

MATERIALS:

• Bible

• Pictures of the Last Supper (see church library, city library, etc.) These can be photographed and shown as slides if desired.

• Paper, crayons, paint etc.

"Thou Preparest A Table Before Me"

MAIN IDEA: Christ, as our Shepherd, prepared a "table for us", the Lord's Supper, as a reminder of his life, love and spirit freely given for us.

SCRIPTURE: Psalm 23

BACKGROUND: Throughout the 23rd Psalm David compares God to a good shepherd who conscienciously cares for His flock. The more we understand about shepherding in Biblical times, the more we appreciate David's relationship with God.

Every year before the flocks journeyed to the high plateau, or tableland as it was called, the shepherd and his family went ahead to prepare the pastures for them by placing salt and other necessary minerals in strategic locations and by destroying poisonous plants before the sheep arrived.

As we think about the preparations that God has made in our behalf, we are reminded of many Old Testament stories, and prophets, but the life of Christ represents God's supreme effort to prepare mankind for eternal life. Jesus lived life as a man and yet also as the Son of God. He did indeed prepare a table for us, the Lord's Supper, as a reminder of his Life, Love and Spirit freely given for us—a lasting symbol of God's boundless Love.

LEARNING ACTIVITIES:

• See filmstrip, "Shepherds in Bible Lands"[1] 5 minutes.

• Discuss the shepherd's responsibilities to the sheep.

• Introduce David as a shepherd who wrote about God as his shepherd. Read the 23rd Psalm.

• If time permits, discuss all the verses and relate them to the filmstrip. If not, concentrate on the meaning of verse 5 and relate it to the Lord's Supper.

• Pass out bookmarks with the 23rd Psalm on them.

• Close with prayer.

MATERIALS:

• Bible

• 23rd Psalm bookmarks

• Projector, screen

[1]Filmstrip "Shepherds in Bible Lands" from the series, *Daily Life in Bible Lands*, by Family Filmstrips. Available from Alba House Communications, Canfield, OH, 44406.

LESSON 18

"The True Vine"

MAIN IDEA: Through Communion, Christ becomes a part of us, and gives us New Life.

SCRIPTURE: John 15:1-17 Jesus the True Vine

LEARNING ACTIVITIES:

• Have the youth examine several grape vines, some living, with leaves and grapes; some dried and dead. Taste some grapes.

• Discuss how the vines are tended and pruned so that they will produce more fruit. The barren branches are cut and burned. Pruning is done in the winter, when the vine is dormant.

• Because there were many vineyards in Palestine, the people were familiar with tending vines, so Jesus used the story of the true vine to help them understand what it meant to live in his love.

• Have the young people read and discuss the verses. How do we know if we abide in him?   What is the core of existence with Christ?   (Love God and one another)

• Communion is another way that we share our "oneness" with Christ and one another. Discuss.

• Sing, "His Banner Over Us is Love". One of the verses is as follows: *"He is the vine and we are the branches, and the banner over us is Love."*

• Use body movements with song. Stand straight and tall with hands at your sides as you sing "He is the Vine"; reach out with your arms and legs as you sing, "we are the branches". Both hands are held together over your head for "the banner" and are placed over the heart as you sing "Love".

• Close with prayer.

MATERIALS:

• Bibles   • Grapes and vines, pruning shears

R. S. V. P.

MAIN IDEA: Christ invites us to share LIFE in him, and we must R.S.V.P. in some way.

SCRIPTURE: Luke 14:15-24 "...*Come, for all is now ready...*"

LEARNING ACTIVITIES:

• Discuss inviting friends to dinner or to a party. How did you help prepare for the party? How did you feel when your guest answered "yes", or "no" to your invitation?

• Have the young people read the Bible verses and briefly discuss the symbolism in the parable. See Lesson IX. Discuss the way different people responded to the invitation with excuses.

• Show sample invitations which contain an R.S.V.P. Discuss what R.S.V.P. means and various ways of responding; phone, note, etc.

• Distribute invitations for Communion and life with Christ. Jesus has invited us to a special meal, Communion, because he loves us. He wants us to remember him, and to know that he is always with us. He wants us to know we are his friends.

• How do we R.S.V.P. an invitation from God?

• On the back of the invitations have the youth write an R.S.V.P. to God's invitation in the form of a prayer. It may include some way of giving themselves, some sort of action e.g. a commitment to prayer, study, worship, kindness toward others, etc. It may be a simple "Yes, Lord, I'll come."

• Have the young people take their invitations to the sanctuary and place them in the offering plates during the offering. This will help reinforce the offering as "giving something to God."

• Close with prayer.

MATERIALS:

• Bibles   • Invitations, pencils

"The Communion of Saints"
(Worldwide Communion Sunday)

MAIN IDEA: The observance of Worldwide Communion on the first Sunday of October provides an excellent opportunity to emphasize the common bond we share through Christ, with Christians around the world.

SCRIPTURE: 1 Corinthians 12-26 Unity in diversity, many members of one body.

LEARNING ACTIVITIES:

• Have the young people read the Bible verses in 1 Corinthians 12.

• Briefly discuss differences in customs, traditions, etc. of various denominations and reinforce the words of Paul, that we are one in Christ. This "oneness" we celebrate together on Worldwide Communion Sunday. We are not alone in our worship of Christ, we share it with believers worldwide.

• Have the youth make final preparations for a "Breaking Bread Together Brunch" for the congregation to follow the Communion service.

• Tables can be decorated with brightly colored cloths. Centerpieces can suggest people from around the world and Communion. Small dolls from different countries, clusters of grapes, and sheaves of wheat are a few ideas.

• The menu can consist of small loaves of bread from around the world and fruit juice.

• The bread can be served on small breadboards with a Communion picture decoupaged to it. These can be taken home for each family as a further reminder of the meaning of Worldwide Communion Sunday.

  • Making the breadboards is a good project for an older elementary or jr. high group to do ahead of time. (See Learning Activities)

  • Boards can be cut from pine, or small ready-made breadboards can be purchased. Church bulletins provide excellent Communion pictures to decoupage.

MATERIALS:

- Bibles

- Table cloths

- Table decorations

- Bread

- Juice

"Communion Word Search"

MAIN IDEA: This is an extension activity which will further familiarize young people with Communion terms and will reinforce the biblical adage, "Seek and ye shall find..."

SCRIPTURE: Matthew 7:7 *"Seek and ye shall find..."*

LEARNING ACTIVITIES:

• Have the youth define the words printed at the top of the word search page to make sure they have an understanding of each, and its relation to Communion.

• Have the youth find the Communion words hidden on the page and remind them that just as they search for the hidden words, so they must continue to search for a deeper meaning in life which can be found through fellowship with Christ.

MATERIALS:

• Word search sheets

• Pencils

COMMUNION WORD SEARCH

Define the following words and tell how each relates to Communion. Circle the words hidden in the word search below. Words are found horizontally, vertically, and diagonally.

BIBLE	DISCIPLE	MATTHEW
BLOOD	DO THIS	REMEMBRANCE
BODY	EUCHARIST	SACRAMENT
BREAD	HYMN	SHEAF
BROKEN	JESUS	SHED
CHALICE	LUKE	TABLE
CHRIST	LORD	TWELVE
COMMUNION	LORD'S SUPPER	WINE
COVENANT	MARK	WHEAT

C	H	C	O	V	E	N	A	N	T	T	W	E	L	V	E
R	I	E	U	C	H	A	R	I	S	T	I	B	O	D	Y
I	B	L	O	O	D	M	E	O	A	U	L	O	R	D	T
S	I	T	O	M	I	A	M	O	C	R	I	C	D	K	M
D	B	H	Y	M	N	T	E	B	R	E	A	D	S	B	E
I	L	L	O	U	E	T	M	T	A	B	L	E	S	R	S
S	E	W	I	N	E	H	B	E	M	A	R	K	U	O	J
C	H	A	L	I	C	E	R	I	E	D	O	N	P	K	E
I	H	E	I	O	H	W	A	S	N	M	N	E	P	E	S
P	C	R	D	N	E	S	N	H	T	A	I	S	E	N	U
L	O	V	I	G	W	A	C	E	L	U	K	E	R	S	S
E	H	E	M	S	W	H	E	A	T	D	O	T	H	I	S
D	A	R	C	H	T	E	T	F	S	M	O	P	W	R	D

"In Case Of Doubt"

MAIN IDEA: The Communion reminds us that Jesus is always with us, even amid our doubts. He is eager to strengthen our faith and lead us onward.

SCRIPTURE: John 20:19-31 Thomas doubts and then believes.

LEARNING ACTIVITIES:

• Briefly review the events of Easter morning: the empty tomb, two men meeting Jesus on the road to Emmaus, Jesus appearing to the 11 disciples

• Have the young people imagine that they were in Jerusalem at the time and had heard rumors of Jesus' resurrection. What would their reaction to the news be? Would they be quick to believe, or would they have doubts? Discuss some of their doubts.

• Read the story of Thomas in the Bible, John 20:19-31.

• Jesus is always with us—even when we doubt. He waits patiently for us to realize his presence. His love and support are always there to remove our doubts and strengthen our faith.

• When we gather as a congregation to celebrate the Lord's Supper, we share the love of Christ and remember his promise to always be with us. We help strengthen and affirm one another's faith.

• Communion is a very real way of experiencing God's love. Have the youth sing "Pass it On" and think about the meaning of the words as they sing, especially the last verse. This must have been the way that Thomas felt after he had seen Jesus.

• Close with prayer.

MATERIALS:

• Bibles

• Words and music to "Pass it On"

"A Forgiven People"

MAIN IDEA: The Communion is a celebration of the forgiveness we know through Christ.

SCRIPTURE: Luke 15:11-32 The Prodigal Son.

LEARNING ACTIVITIES:

• Discuss what it means to be forgiven. Have the youth share experiences where they have done something wrong and then been forgiven.

• Discuss how you felt when you knew you had made a mistake. When you had been forgiven. How did you know that you were forgiven?

• Introduce the story of the Prodigal Son and encourage the youth to think about how the father and the younger son felt throughout the story.

• Read the parable.

• Discuss the feelings of the father and the son especially during the homecoming and the celebration. Jesus told this story to show us the greatness of God's love, and how willing He is to forgive us.

• The Communion reminds us that Jesus gave his life freely to show us even more clearly that God loves and forgives us. Matthew 26:28 "...*for this is my blood of the covenant which is poured out for many for the forgiveness of sins.*"

• The Communion service is a celebration, like that of the father and the son in the story. Through the Communion we celebrate or "togetherness" with God and one another.

• Close with prayer.

MATERIALS:

• Bibles

LESSON 24

"A Labor of Love"

MAIN IDEA: Jesus gave his life willingly for us. Let us return his love by giving our lives and our work to him. Let all that we do be done by the glory of God.

SCRIPTURE: Romans 12:1-8 *"I appeal to you therefore, brethren, by the mercies of God, to present your bodies as a living sacrifice, holy and acceptable to God...Having gifts that differ according to the grace given to us, let us use them..."*

Colossians 3:23 *"Whatever your task, work heartily, as serving the Lord and not men..."*

I Corinthians 10:31 *"...Whatever you do, do all to the glory of God."*

LEARNING ACTIVITIES:

• Distribute pictures which show people of all ages involved in some sort of work. Remember that play is very important "work" for children. They learn a great deal about life through their play. Some pictures can be of work in Bible times.

• Discuss the various types of work shown in the pictures and the kinds of work the children and their parents do.

• Read one or more of the Bible verses which tell us something very important about the work we do.

• Examine how Jesus lived his life. He didn't hold anything back. He gave his all, his life, to demonstrate the greatness of God's love for us.

• Discuss ways that we can "do our work to the Glory of God".

• Have the youth draw a small picture which illustrates some work they do each day. These can be placed in the offering plates during the service to further reinforce the idea of doing their work for God.

MATERIALS:

- Bibles

- Pictures of people at work

- Paper and crayons

SECTION 2

COMMUNION SERVICES

World-wide Communion Sunday

WORLD WIDE COMMUNION:

This is a Communion service designed to emphasize the common bond which all Christians around the world share through Christ and his institution of the Lord's Supper.

BEFORE THE SERVICE:

Assemble a collection of slides which show: people of all ages from every part of the world, church buildings and scenes of people receiving Communion in varied settings. Slides of various artists' renditions of the Last Supper will help unify the presentation and reemphasize the reason we are all gathered together this day.

The slides can be made by photographing books or magazine pictures with a close-up lens. Making and organizing the slides can involve pastors, worship committees, teachers, and the young people.

Set up projector and screen. Check equipment and make arrangements to darken the sanctuary.

CALL TO WORSHIP:

PASTOR:

WE HAVE BEEN INVITED TO WORSHIP AND TO GATHER AROUND THIS TABLE TO CELEBRATE OUR ONENESS WITH GOD AND ONE ANOTHER.

PEOPLE:

WE COME AS ONE PEOPLE TO WORSHIP AND PRAISE THE LORD OUR GOD, AND TO RECEIVE THE BLESSING OF HIS PRESENCE.

UNISON:

COME, LET US WORSHIP AND REJOICE IN THE LORD!

PRAYER OF CONFESSION: *(Unison)*

FATHER, TOO OFTEN WE FOCUS OUR ATTENTION ON OURSELVES AND NOT ON YOU. TOO OFTEN WE CENTER OUR LIVES AROUND OUR OWN WANTS AND DESIRES WITHOUT THOUGHT OF YOU OR THE NEEDS OF OTHERS. FORGIVE US FOR OUR SHORTSIGHTEDNESS AND OPEN OUR EYES THAT WE MAY BE GUIDED BY YOUR LOVING SPIRIT. THROUGH JESUS CHRIST OUR LORD. AMEN.

ASSURANCE OF PARDON: *(Pastor)*

LET US REJOICE AND BE GLAD, FOR GOD HEARS HIS CHILDREN AND BY HIS GRACE HAS SAVED US FROM OUR SIN. AMEN.

SUGGESTED SCRIPTURE:

I Corinthians 10:17 *"Because there is one bread, we who are many are one body, for we all partake of the one bread."*

COMMUNION MEDITATION:

Some of the slides may be shown during the meditation as a way of visually stating the message.

THE SACRAMENT OF THE LORD'S SUPPER:

The remainder of the slides can be shown as the Sacrament is being served. This will further reinforce the significance of World Wide Communion.

FOOLISH FOR CHRIST

CHRISTIANS, CLOWNS, AND COMMUNION:

A Communion experience designed to illustrate the risks involved in being a Christian, and the support and purpose that is offered to each person through fellowship and Communion within the Church.

BEFORE THE SERVICE:

• Decorate pews and sanctuary with balloons.

• Fill enough helium balloons for the entire congregation, and hide them in a nearby room.

• Set up projector and screen in sanctuary. Test equipment. Film: "A Clown is Born".

• Have someone dressed as a clown hidden and ready to assist with the service.

CALL TO WORSHIP:

PASTOR:
COME, LET US REJOICE AND BE GLAD, FOR GOD HAS CALLED US TO BE HIS PEOPLE.

PEOPLE:
WE COME THIS MORNING BRINGING OUR PRAYERS AND VOICES LIFTED IN SONGS OF PRAISE TO GOD, OUR FATHER THROUGH HIS SON JESUS CHRIST OUR LORD.

PRAYER OF CONFESSION: *(Unison)*

FATHER, FOR ALL THE TIMES WE KEPT SILENT WHEN WE COULD HAVE SHARED YOUR WORDS OF LOVE AND REASSURANCE WITH SOMEONE WHO NEEDED THEM,

FORGIVE US. FOR THE TIMES WE TURNED OUR BACKS INSTEAD OF THE OTHER CHEEK, FATHER FORGIVE US. FOR THE TIMES WE WITHDREW OUR FRIENDSHIP INSTEAD OF EXTENDING OUR HAND TO A NEIGHBOR, FATHER FORGIVE US.

ASSURANCE OF PARDON: *(Pastor)*

CHRIST HAS PROMISED ETERNAL LIFE TO ALL WHO BELIEVE IN HIM. LET US REJOICE IN HIS GRACE AND GO FORTH AS NEW CREATURES, FILLED WITH HIS LOVE AND ALLOWING HIS SPIRIT TO LIVE THROUGH OUR LIVES.

SUGGESTED SCRIPTURE:

Matthew 16:25,26 *"Whoever would save his life will lose it and whoever loses his life for my sake will find it. For what will it profit a man if he gains the whole world and loses his soul?"*

I Corinthians 4:10-13 *"We are fools for Christ's sake..."*

Galatians 2:20 *"I have been crucified with Christ: it is no longer I who live, but Christ who lives in me; and the life I now live in the flesh I live by faith in the Son of God, who loved me and gave himself for me."*

COMMUNION   MEDITATION: BECOMING FOOLISH FOR CHRIST

INTRODUCTION:

So often we "tune out" and "turn off" the world outside and go through life without experiencing its richness and depth. We operate only on the surface of things. Because the film is non-verbal, it challenges us to use our other senses to discover its meaning.

ENCOURAGE THEM TO:

• Look for meaning in the actions/symbols presented.

• Look for examples of rejection, humiliation, resurrection, joy and other feelings that the clown experiences.

• Think about the risks that the clown takes and why.

SHOW FILM: "A Clown is Born"

BRIEF DISCUSSION:

• Recap the clowns' various jobs and experiences.

• Describe the experience within the church and its effect on both clowns.

• What is the significance of the balloons?

• How can we relate the clowns' experiences to our own?

THE SACRAMENT OF THE LORD'S SUPPER:

COMMUNION HYMN: "Take My Life and Let It Be "

• During the Communion hymn a clown wanders into the sanctuary and is invited to the Communion table. He will assist in serving the Communion by breaking the bread and pouring the wine as done in the film.

• Use one large loaf of bread for the entire congregation as was done in the film.

AFTER FILM AND COMMUNION, READ "RISK" IN UNISON:

"RISK"

To laugh is to risk appearing a fool.
To weep is to risk appearing sentimental.
To reach out for another is to risk involvement.
To expose feelings is to risk exposing your true self.
To place your ideas, your dreams before the crowd is to risk their loss.
To love is to risk not being loved in return.
To live is to risk dying.
To hope is to risk despair.
To try is to risk failure.

But risks must be taken because the greatest hazard in life is to risk nothing. The person who risks nothing does nothing, has nothing, is nothing. He may avoid suffering and sorrow, but he simply cannot learn, feel, change, grow, love...live. Chained by his certitudes, he is a slave; he has forfeited freedom. Only a person who risks is free.

Author Unknown

HYMN OF RESPONSE: "So Let Your Lips and Lives Express" or "Open My Eyes That I May See"

During closing hymn have clown pass out balloons to everyone. Following the benediction, the congregation can go outside and let their balloons go into the community. (Symbolic of unleashing Christian love into the world.)

"A Clown is Born" 16mm film, 15 minutes.
Produced by Faith and Fantasy, Inc. and available through Mass Media Ministries, 2116 North Charles St., Baltimore, Maryland 21228. Rental $25.00.

For more information on Clown Ministry, refer to:

THE COMPLETE FLOYD SHAFFER CLOWN MINISTRY
    WORKSHOP KIT.

        Produced by Dennis C. Benson
        P.O. Box 12811
        Pittsburgh, PA 15241
        Available through Cokesbury

Getting To Know You

KOINONIA: FELLOWSHIP

A Communion experience designed to encourage the congregation to look beyond their individual needs and strengthen bonds with one another through Christ.

CALL TO WORSHIP:

PASTOR:

JESUS SAID, "COME TO ME ALL WHO ARE HEAVY LADEN, AND I WILL GIVE YOU REST."

UNISON:

COME LET US WORSHIP WITH SONG AND PRAYER. LET US REJOICE IN THE STEADFAST LOVE AND MERCY OF THE LORD OUR GOD.

PRAYER OF CONFESSION: *(Unison)*

OUR FATHER, AGAIN WE COME INTO YOUR PRESENCE BURDENED WITH OUR PRIVATE WORRIES AND FEARS. FORGIVE US FOR BEING SO SHORTSIGHTED THAT WE MISS THE JOY AND REASSURANCE OF YOUR PRESENCE IN OUR LIVES. OPEN OUR EYES AND HEARTS TO THE NEEDS OF THOSE AROUND US AND HELP US RESPOND TO THEM WITH YOUR LOVE, THROUGH CHRIST JESUS OUR LORD. AMEN.

ASSURANCE OF PARDON: *(Pastor)*

CHRIST CAME INTO THE WORLD TO GIVE SIGHT TO THE BLIND. RECEIVE THE GOOD NEWS OF GOD'S LOVE AND FORGIVENESS FOR YOU AND RESPOND WITH JOY AND CARING FOR ONE ANOTHER.

SUGGESTED SCRIPTURE:

I Corinthians 12:12-13 *"Just as the body has many parts, so it is with the 'body' of Christ."*

Matthew 13:1-17 Parable of the sower *"...He who has ears let him hear."*

I Corinthians 10:17 *"Because there is one bread, we who are many are one body, for we all partake of the one bread."*

COMMUNION MEDITATION: KOINONIA

INTRODUCTION:

We more often than not approach Communion with thoughts and prayers about ourselves and our personal relationship with Christ. This morning we are going to focus our attention on one another and share our concerns as we come to the Communion table.

Encourage people to REALLY LISTEN to one another. Keep conversations moving and brief. This is not in depth therapy, it is a "getting to know you" experience.

CONGREGATION ACTIVITY: Directed conversations

• Ask people to change seats and sit beside someone they don't know, or would like to get to know better. (Groups of 2 or 3.)

• Pass out name tags and felt pens. Have people make a name tag for their partner using their full name.

• Tell your partner something about your name, what does it mean? What country is it from? Were you named after someone?

• Find out what your partner does for a living, how they spend their spare time. (Favorite hobbies, talents etc.)

• Share your hopes and plans for the near future.

• Share a recent, happy experience.

• Share a recent sorrow.

• Share your greatest concern for either yourself, your family, community, church, or nation.

COMMUNION HYMN: "The Light of God is Falling"

THE SACRAMENT OF THE LORD'S SUPPER:

• When serving the congregation, instruct elders to serve each group who will in turn, serve one another saying their name as they serve the elements.

49

IN RESPONSE TO COMMUNION:

• Read the "PRAYER OF ST. FRANCIS" in unison.

> *"Lord, make me an instrument of Thy peace.*
> *Where there is hatred, let me sow love;*
> *Where there is doubt, faith;*
> *Where there is darkness, light;*
> *Where there is sadness, joy.*
>
> *O Divine, Master, grant that I may not so much seek*
> *To be consoled, as to console;*
> *Not so much to be understood as*
> *to understand; not so much to be*
> *Loved as to love.*
>
> *For it is in giving that we receive;*
> *It is in pardoning, that we are pardoned;*
> *It is in dying, that we awaken to eternal life."*

HYMN OF RESPONSE: "Blest Be The Tie That Binds"

Maundy Thursday

AGAPE COMMUNION (A Maundy Thursday evening experience)

Early Christians often met together to share a common meal called the Agape Feast. Sharing food unselfishly with one another was one way they practiced "loving your brother and your neighbor." This Agape meal always ended with the celebration of the Lord's Supper.

Turn a pot-luck dinner, or pot-luck dessert into an Agape Communion experience for Maundy Thursday.

GETTING READY:

• In a fellowship hall, arrange tables in a large "C" shape, with a small Communion table in the center. If more seating is needed, arrange tables around the Communion table like the spokes of a wheel.

• Emphasize the theme of the evening with posters, pictures and other wall decorations which illustrate the Last Supper and other events of Holy Week. Let the church school help with the decorations.

• Cover each table with a white tablecloth and have a 6 inch strip of purple crepe paper running lengthwise in the center of each table.

• Have at least two purple candles on each table, as candlelight will serve as the only light during the service.

• Decorate the tables with as many symbols of Holy Week, and Communion as you can find. Involve groups within the congregation to help. Here are some suggestions:

• Torn curtain	• Palm leaf
• Sponge and vinegar	• Grapes
• Wooden cross	• Loaf of bread
• Large rusty nails	• Unleavened bread
• Thorn crown	• Lamb

- Chalice
- Wine bottle
- Sheaf of wheat
- Toy donkey
- Rock

- Dice
- Bowl and towel
- Alabaster vase
- 30 silver coins
- Bibles

- Have small glasses available on serving trays to be distributed following the meal at the beginning of the service.

THE AGAPE MEAL:

- During the meal encourage people to examine the symbols on the tables and share their meaning with one another.

- Following the meal the small glasses are distributed to everyone.

COMMUNION MEDITATION:

SERVING THE SACRAMENT:

- Use a single loaf of bread and pour the wine (grape juice) into each person's glass individually. Ask that everyone wait to partake until all have been served.

- Close with a hymn and prayer.

SERVICE 5

Let The Little Ones Come

COMMUNION: CHILDREN'S DIALOGUE

In an effort to share our young people's understanding of Communion with the whole congregation, have a class discussion about the Last Supper and Communion and record it. Questions and the children's answers to them are then written on 3x5'' cards and serve as the script for a dialogue between the youth. This dialogue becomes part of the invitation to the sacrament.

BEFORE THE SERVICE:

Have the youth practice reading their dialogue at the front of the sanctuary and "walk through" their part of the service.

CALL TO WORSHIP:

PASTOR:

CHILDREN OF GOD, BOTH YOUNG AND OLD, LET US JOIN TOGETHER AND WORSHIP THE LORD OUR GOD.

UNISON:

LET US BRING TO HIM OUR SINGING, OUR PRAYERS, OUR HOPES AND FEARS. LET US GATHER AT HIS TABLE AND REJOICE IN HIS PRESENCE.

PRAYER OF CONFESSION: (UNISON)

WE COME BEFORE YOU, OUR FATHER, AS LITTLE CHILDREN, WIDE EYED AND AWED BY YOUR PRESENCE. WE ARE FILLED WITH QUESTIONS AND UNCERTAINTIES ABOUT OUR LIVES, AND WE SEARCH IN ALL THE WRONG PLACES FOR ANSWERS. FORGIVE US, FOR FORGETTING TO TURN TO YOU FOR TRUTH, LORD, AND GRANT US THE REASURRANCE OF YOUR LOVE AND THE PRESENCE OF YOUR SPIRIT, IN CHRIST'S NAME WE PRAY. AMEN.

ASSURANCE OF PARDON: (PASTOR)

JESUS SAID, "BRING THE LITTLE CHILDREN TO ME FOR OF SUCH IS THE KINGDOM OF HEAVEN." RECEIVE THE BLESSING OF GOD'S LOVE AND FORGIVENESS GIVEN FREELY THROUGH HIS SON OUR LORD.

SUGGESTED SCRIPTURE:

Luke 18:16-17 *"Let the children come to me..."*

Matthew 18:1-6 *"...unless you turn and become like children..."*

COMMUNION MEDITATION: BECOMING CHILDREN OF GOD

COMMUNION HYMN: "Here, O My Lord, I See Thee Face to Face"

THE SACRAMENT OF THE LORD'S SUPPER:

CHILDREN PRESENT COMMUNION DIALOGUE: (Sample below, let your children write their own.)

Q. Why do we celebrate the Lord's Supper?

A. Jesus told us to do it so that we would remember him.

Q. What did Jesus do at the Last Supper?

A. He got up from the table and washed his disciples' feet to show them that he was willing to serve them, and they should be willing to serve one another. No job is too small to be done with love.

Q. What else did Jesus do that night?

A. He took some bread and broke it and said, "This is my body broken for you." When we eat the bread during Communion, we remember that Jesus gave his life willingly to show us how great God's love really is.

PASTOR: *(Breaks bread and gives trays to children who will serve the congregation.)*

CHILDREN'S DIALOGUE CONTINUES:

Q. What else did Jesus do at the Supper?

A. He told his disciples that when they drank the wine it would remind them of his blood, shed for them.

Q. Why do you use such small cups for Communion?

A. Communion isn't an ordinary meal. It's something special, and it only takes a little to remind us of all that Christ did for us.

PASTOR: *(Pours wine and gives trays to children who will serve the congregation.)*

Q. If Communion is so important, why don't we have it every week?

A. We want it to always be something special and we don't want to take it for granted.

HYMN OF RESPONSE: "A Parting Hymn We Sing"

A Communion Play

COMMUNION DRAMA:

Have you ever imagined what it would have been like to be sittir with the disciples at the Last Supper? Your congregation can have thi experience through a Communion Drama. Use older students or adults fo speaking parts. If your denomination requires an ordained person to administer the sacrament, he or she can be part of the dramatization.

BEFORE THE SERVICE:

• Set up a long table in front of the sanctuary with several folding chairs around it.

• Have the youth practice their lines and "walk through" the service.

CALL TO WORSHIP:

PASTOR:
OPEN YOUR EYES AND YOUR HEARTS. LET YOUR EARS HEAR THE WORDS OF THE LORD, AND MAY YOUR SOUL BE NOURISHED BY THE FOOD AT HIS TABLE.

PEOPLE:
WE GATHER AROUND THE LORD'S TABLE WITH THANKSGIVING AND WITH THE EXPECTATION THAT HIS LOVING SPIRIT WILL FILL OUR LIVES.

PRAYER OF CONFESSION: (UNISON)

LORD, WE CALL OURSELVES CHRISTIAN WHEN SO OFTEN WE TURN OUR BACKS ON YOU AND OUR NEIGHBOR. WE WITHHOLD THE LOVE THAT YOU GIVE SO FREELY. WE ARE SILENT WHEN YOUR SPIRIT URGES US TO SPEAK. WE BLURT OUT WORDS AND LATER WISH WE'D KEPT SILENT. WE FEEL SORRY FOR OURSELVES INSTEAD OF REACHING OUT WITH COMPASSION FOR OUR NEIGHBOR. FORGIVE US OUR FATHER. RENEW OUR DISCIPLESHIP AND SEND US INTO OUR WORLD WITH THE REASSURANCE OF YOUR PRESENCE AND THE STRENGTH OF YOUR ETERNAL LOVE. AMEN.

ASSURANCE OF PARDON: (PASTOR)

EVEN THOUGH THEY DESERTED HIM, JESUS STILL LOVED THEM. HE DIED ON THE CROSS AND RETURNED TO HIS DISCIPLES TO REASSURE THEM OF HIS CONTINUING LOVE AND PRESENCE WITH THEM. "I WILL NOT LEAVE YOU DESOLATE," HE SAID, AND NEITHER WILL HE LEAVE US ALONE. RECEIVE GOD'S LOVE AND FORGIVENESS GIVEN FREELY TO YOU THROUGH OUR LORD JESUS CHRIST. AMEN.

SCRIPTURE: Matthew 26:17-25

COMMUNION MEDITATION: "Not I, Lord!"

THE SACRAMENT OF THE LORD'S SUPPER:

DISCIPLE 1: (from the back of the sanctuary) This is the place, the room where we are to prepare the Passover meal. Come, help me get ready.

(The disciples come forward with final preparations for the Lord's Supper: chairs, cloth, bread, wine, chalice, and pitcher. Jesus follows.)

(Jesus and disciples are seated around the Communion table in costume.)

DISCIPLE 2. What makes this Passover meal different from all the others we've celebrated together?

JESUS: This will be our last Passover together until it is fulfilled in the Kingdom of God.

DISCIPLE 3: But why must you die?

JESUS: Greater love has no man than to lay down his life for his friends, and you are all my friends. And this is my commandment, that you love one another as I have loved you.

(Jesus stands and takes the bread and breaks it, giving a piece to each disciple, saying...)

JESUS: This is my body which is broken for you. Do this in remembrance of me.

(Jesus then gives bread to the disciples who serve the congregation. Jesus sits while they are being served.)

(When disciples return and are seated, Jesus stands, slowly pours the wine into the chalice and says:)

JESUS: This wine is the new covenant sealed with my blood. Drink this in remembrance of me.

(Jesus gives trays to disciples who serve the congregation. Disciples are served when they return. Everyone partakes together.)

JESUS: Whenever you tell this story, whenever you bless and share this bread and wine, you will be doing more than just remembering; I will be with you. I will become a part of you and you will draw new life from me, like the fruit draws its life from the tree. Let us sing a hymn of praise to God, our Father.

ALL DISCIPLES: (TOGETHER) Amen!

(The youth move to front pews for remainder of service.)

Give Us This Day

OUR DAILY BREAD

This is a Communion service designed to expand the congregation's understanding of the phrase "give us this day, our daily bread", and relate it to the Communion experience.

BEFORE THE SERVICE:

Prepare small individually wrapped loaves of bread, one per family. These will be distributed at the end of the worship service. Members of the congregation may help bake the bread.

CALL TO WORSHIP:

PASTOR:
JESUS SAID, "I AM THE BREAD OF LIFE. HE WHO COMES TO ME WILL NEVER HUNGER."

PEOPLE:
"BLESSED ARE THEY WHO HUNGER AND THIRST FOR RIGHTEOUSNESS' SAKE, FOR THEY SHALL BE FILLED."

UNISON:
COME, LET US SEEK THE LORD, THAT WE MAY KNOW THE TRUTH OF HIS WORDS AND THE FULLNESS OF HIS PRESENCE.

PRAYER OF CONFESSION: (UNISON)

WE HUNGER FOR MANY THINGS, OUR FATHER, FINANCIAL AND MATERIAL SUCCESS, ACCEPTANCE AND POPULARITY AMONG OUR PEERS, THINGS THAT IN THE LONG RUN, DON'T REALLY MATTER. FORGIVE US, AND HELP US, WE PRAY, TO SEEK YOU AND YOUR KINGDOM FIRST, REMEMBERING THAT YOU KNOW OUR REAL NEEDS, EVEN BEFORE WE ASK. CREATE WITHIN US A HUNGER FOR YOUR PRESENCE IN OUR LIVES, AND GRANT THAT IT MAY BE SATISFIED THROUGH CHRIST JESUS OUR LORD. AMEN.

WORDS OF ASSURANCE: (PASTOR)

SEEK AND YOU SHALL FIND. KNOCK AND IT SHALL BE OPENED. ASK AND IT SHALL BE GIVEN UNTO YOU. RECEIVE THE LOVE AND FORGIVENESS OF GOD, FREELY GIVEN THROUGH HIS SON, JESUS CHRIST OUR LORD. AMEN.

COMMUNION MEDITATION: "Give Us This Day, Our Daily Bread..."

VARIOUS INTERPRETATIONS OF THE PHRASE:

1. Bread of the Lord's Supper.

2. Spiritual food of God's Word.

3. Jesus, the Bread of Life.

4. The Messianic banquet.

The exact meaning of the Greek word, "epiousious", was not known until the word was found on a fragment of a Greek shopping list. Thus it is a simple prayer that God will supply us with the things we need for the coming day.

TRUTHS THAT EMERGE AS A RESULT OF THIS DISCOVERY:

1. God is concerned with our whole salvation; body, mind, and spirit, not just soul.

2. Live one day at a time. Trust God. Don't be anxious about tomorrow.

3. It teaches us to SHARE OUR DAILY BREAD.

SACRAMENT OF THE LORD'S SUPPER:

Serve the Sacrament using a single loaf.

PRAYER OF RESPONSE:

The Lord's Prayer.

OFFERTORY:

Following the offering, distribute the loaves of bread to each family and encourage them to "break bread" and share the love of Christ with someone during the coming week.

Love Made Manifest

LABOR OF LOVE

This is a Communion experience which brings Christ into the daily lives and work of the congregation.

BEFORE THE SERVICE:

Have someone take slides of as many members of the congregation as possible at their weekly jobs. Photograph those who are retired or work at home, too. Assemble slides and have them ready to share with the congregation during the service.

CALL TO WORSHIP:

PASTOR:
THE LORD CALLS ALL MEN TO WORSHIP HIM AND LIVE IN THE FELLOWSHIP OF HIS LOVE.

PEOPLE:
WE COME TO THIS PLACE IN ANSWER TO HIS CALL. WE SEEK HIS PRESENCE AND BOUNDLESS GRACE THAT WE MAY KNOW ETERNAL LIFE.

PRAYER OF CONFESSION: (UNISON)

OUR FATHER, WE COME INTO YOUR PRESENCE THIS DAY WEARY FROM THE WORK OF THE WEEK, THE CARES AND PRESSURES OF EACH DAY. TOO OFTEN WE HAVE FORGOTTEN THAT YOU PROMISE TO BE ALWAYS A PART OF OUR LIVES. YOUR LOVE AND GRACE ARE ALWAYS PRESENT, BUT WE CHOOSE TO IGNORE THEM AND BROOD IN OUR FRUSTRATIONS AND FEARS. AWAKEN YOUR SPIRIT WITHIN US AND GRANT THAT WE MAY LIVE EACH DAY IN THE FULLNESS OF YOUR LOVE. IN JESUS' NAME WE PRAY. AMEN.

ASSURANCE OF PARDON:

REJOICE, AND KNOW THAT GOD'S PROMISE IS TRUE. HE IS WITH YOU ALWAYS AND HIS SPIRIT IS MADE KNOWN THROUGH THE LIVES AND WORKS OF THOSE WHO LOVE HIM. LET ALL THAT YOU DO BE TO THE GLORY OF GOD.

SUGGESTED SCRIPTURE:

Romans 12:1-8 *"I appeal to you therefore, brethern, by the mercies of God, to present your bodies as a living sacrifice, holy and acceptable to God,.... Having gifts that differ according to the grace given to us, let us use them..."*

Colossians 3:23 *"Whatever your task, work heartily, as serving the Lord and not men..."*

1 Corinthians 10:31 *"...Whatever you do, do all to the glory of God."*

CHILDREN'S MEDITATION:

Show a collection of hats that represent various kinds of work and play. Ask children what kind of work their parents do, and what the children do all day. Play is a child's WORK. God has given us all different skills and interests. He wants us to try our best at whatever we're doing. And to try to please Him in all that we do.

COMMUNION MEDITATION: "A Labor of Love"

COMMUNION HYMN: "Come Labor On"

SACRAMENT OF THE LORD'S SUPPER:

OFFERTORY:

Following the offering set aside time for personal reflection and prayer as the slides of the congregation at work are shown. Encourage people to think about how they can take Christ into their work. Pray for one another as they pursue various jobs.

Communion At Christmas

ADVENT COMMUNION

The Advent Communion is a celebration of Christ's coming into our world and the love and joy which his continued presence with us brings.

BEFORE THE SERVICE:

Arrange for the church school to make and distribute "Communion Bells" to the congregation during the service.

CALL TO WORSHIP:

PASTOR:

I BRING YOU GOOD NEWS OF A GREAT JOY WHICH HAS COME TO ALL PEOPLE. FOR TO YOU THIS DAY HAS COME A SAVIOR WHO IS CHRIST THE LORD.

PEOPLE:

COME, LET US WORSHIP HIM IN SPIRIT AND IN TRUTH. LET US RECEIVE THE JOY WHICH IS CHRIST OUR LORD.

PRAYER OF CONFESSION: (UNISON)

DECEMBER IS UPON US AGAIN, OUR FATHER, AND WE OFTEN FIND OURSELVES LOOKING AT THE HOLIDAY SEASON AS A BURDEN, AN ENDLESS LIST OF PREPARATIONS TO MAKE AND GIFTS TO BUY, CARDS TO WRITE AND TREES TO DECORATE. FORGIVE US, GOD, FOR BEING BLIND TO YOUR LOVE WHICH CAME FOR ALL THE WORLD THROUGH YOUR SON, JESUS CHRIST. IN HIS NAME WE PRAY. AMEN.

WORDS OF ASSURANCE: (PASTOR)

CHRIST CAME INTO THE WORLD THAT THE WORLD THROUGH HIM MIGHT BE SAVED. BE UPLIFTED BY HIS LOVE AND PRESENCE WITH YOU, AND MAY YOUR JOY BE FULL.

SUGGESTED SCRIPTURE:

Luke 2:10-11 *"...I bring you good news of a great joy which will come to all people..."*

John 15:7-11 *"...These things I have spoken to you, that my joy may be in you, and that your joy may be full."*

COMMUNION MEDITATION: Good News! God's Gift Has Arrived!

COMMUNION HYMN: "O Little Town of Bethlehem"

During the Communion Hymn have children distribute the Christmas bell corsages to the congregation. (They can be worn throughout Advent.)

THE SACRAMENT OF THE LORD'S SUPPER:

• Read the last two verses of "O Little Town of Bethlehem" as part of the invitation to the Sacrament.

How silently, how silently the wondrous gift is given!
So God imparts to human hearts the blessings of his heaven.
No ear may hear His coming, but in this world of sin,
Where meek souls will receive him, still the dear Christ enters in.

O holy Child of Bethlehem, descend to us, we pray;
Cast out our sin, and enter in, be born in us today.
We hear the Christmas angels the great glad tidings tell;
O come to us, abide with us, our Lord Emmanuel. Amen."

SECTION 3

COMMUNION RELATED
LEARNING ACTIVITIES

ACTIVITY 1

Bread and Grapes Plaque

DIRECTIONS:

Discuss with the youth the elements of Communion, and what they symbolize. Draw from the young people short phrases which express their understanding of Communion, or prayer relating to the sacrament. Show them a sample of a completed plaque. Have them select a phrase they want to use and find the necessary letters. Glue on ½ a basket, grapes and bread leaving room for the letters. Glue the letters in place and allow it to dry. Attach the hanger to the back.

SUGGESTIONS FOR USE:

• Excellent gifts for Christmas, Mother's Day, Father's Day

• Can be given as gifts to shut-ins, pastors, teachers, etc.

MATERIALS:

• Pine boards or shingles approximately 6" x 8".

• Small bunches of plastic grapes

• Dried rolls

• Small 3" baskets cut in half

• Alphabet soup letters

• White glue

• Hangers for the back of the plaque

Breadboards

DIRECTIONS:

Stain the boards with acrylic paint ahead of time or at the beginning of the class. The paint can dry as you discuss the various symbols and words which are illustrated on the bulletin. Tear or cut out the bulletin so it will fit on the board. Apply a coat of Mod-Poge to seal it. Keep working air bubbles out with a brush as it dries.

SUGGESTIONS FOR USE:

• Gifts for congregation on World Wide Communion Sunday.

• Add a loaf of homemade bread and it becomes a reminder of Communion and the presence of Christ throughout the week.

• They can be used to serve a Communion brunch of bread and fruit.

MATERIALS:

• Communion bulletins

• Small breadboards or pine boards cut to bulletin size

• Mod-Poge

• Paint brushes

• Burnt umber acrylic paint

Communion Mosaics

BACKGROUND:

Mosaics and carvings found in the catacombs illustrate many of the symbols used by early Christians. The fish, one of the earliest Christians symbols, was used as a rebus or secret code which identified Christians to one another. The fish is often found atop a three–legged table or with a basket of bread and wine on its back. When it is shown this way, it represents the Lord's Supper. The chalice and loaves of bread can often be found in the mosaics of early Byzantine churches. The cross, the ☧ and A Ω symbols can also be found.

DIRECTIONS:

Discuss the meaning of each symbol and the use of mosaics in the early church. Let the youth choose their favorite symbol. Lightly draw it onto the construction paper and fill in the symbol with colored squares of one color. Choose another color for the background and glue the squares in place. Allow a small space to show between each piece to simulate grout.

SUGGESTIONS FOR USE:

- Decorate the sanctuary or fellowship hall during a Communion service.

- Decorate classroom, doors, homes.

MATERIALS:

- Colored construction paper for background 9'' x 12''

- Construction paper scraps: cut into ¼''-½'' squares

- White glue

- Illustrations of various Communion symbols

- Pictures or examples of mosaics

Symbols of Communion

DIRECTIONS:

Trim the edges off the meat trays to create a flat carving block. Draw a symbol in the styrofoam block with pencil or pen. Remember that lettering must be reversed on the block. Use enough pressure to create a groove in the styrofoam. Spread ink onto the glass and roll with roller until it is evenly applied and makes a sticky sound. Apply ink to styrofoam with the roller. Place paper on top of the block and rub with the palm of the hand. Remove the print and allow it to dry.

SUGGESTIONS FOR USE:

• The meaning of the symbol can be written on the back.

• Assemble a booklet of Communion symbols.

• Special Communion bulletins.

• Folders for Communion study booklets.

• Cards for congregation, "shut-ins"

• Several can be put together to form a banner

• Classroom decoration.

MATERIALS:

• Styrofoam meat trays, egg carton lids or similar material

• Pencils, ballpoint pens

• Newsprint or colored construction paper

• Printing ink, rubber roller and sheet of glass, or,

• Tempera paint, brush

• Illustrations of various Communion symbols

Acrostics

DIRECTIONS:

Acrostics offer a challenging and creative way for young people to express their understanding about Communion. A key word is written vertically along the left side of the page. Its letters become the first letter of the first word for each line of the story. They may choose any of the following terms to use as key words: Communion, Sacrament, Lord's Supper, Eucharist.

Below is a sample acrostic about Communion using the word Jesus.

Just as Jesus and his disciples did at the Last Supper, we
Eat the bread and drink the wine remembering that he loved us
So much that he gave his life freely to show
Us the greatness of God's love. He told us to
Serve and love one another as he has loved us.

SUGGESTIONS FOR USE:

• Bulletin boards

• Cards

• They can be incorporated in the Communion worship service.

MATERIALS:

• Pencils, paper

• Sample acrostic and key words

Communion Preparation

DIRECTIONS:

As part of a Communion study, small groups of young people help the deacons or others prepare the elements for the Lord's Supper. As the bread is broken into small pieces, discuss the meaning of "this is my body broken for you." As the grape juice is poured into the small cups, discuss, "This is the New Covenant of my blood, shed for you." Also discuss how, through prayer, the common elements become holy and sacred. The children can also help set the Communion table at the front of the sanctuary.

SUGGESTIONS FOR USE:

• Prior to a regular Communion service.

• As a learning center experience during an intergenerational event which will end with a Communion service.

• Before a family night agape supper.

MATERIALS:

• Communion ware

• Elements, bread and grape juice

Joyful Banners

DIRECTIONS:

Look at all our Communion symbols and think about what they mean. Think for a moment about what Communion means to YOU. Design a banner which expresses "What Is Most Important About Communion to YOU". Use symbols and words. Make a fold about 2" wide along the top of the colored paper. Fold it toward the back side. Tie yarn in a loop and slip under the top flap. Glue the flap in place, and display banner on the wall.

SUGGESTIONS FOR USE:

• Decorations for sanctuary, fellowship hall, classroom.

• Take home decoration gifts to "shut-ins".

MATERIALS:

• Colored paper (see printers for surplus stock)

• Scissors

• Samples of Communion symbols and patterns (if desired)

• Felt pens

• Paste or glue

• Yarn

Tissue Paper Stained Glass

Communion symbols become the subject of large tissue paper glass panels, which can decorate your sanctuary or fellowship hall.

Creating the panels is an activity that is enjoyed by everyone from preschoolers to adults. The experience is easily adapted to many different learning situations, including church school classes, youth group activities and intergenerational Lenten workshops.

DIRECTIONS:

With pencil LIGHTLY draw the symbol on butcher paper. Divide the background into sections which will be different colors. Cut or tear tissue paper to fit each section. It's OK if some overlap—that helps create a feeling of transparency. To help unify the panels and emphasize the symbol on each one, use lighter pastel colors for the symbols. Apply Mod-Poge to one section at a time and cover with tissue paper.

When the entire window is dry, lightly paint the black lines and print the captions for each symbol. Fasten the finished panels to walls or windows with black electrical tape. These panels can be shown individually or grouped together to create a "stained glass" wall. During the Lenten season, they become especially welcomed decorations for church, home, hospitals, and convalescent nomes.

MATERIALS:

• Butcher paper or craft paper (Approx. 30" x 36")

• Colored tissue paper

• Mod-Poge or similar clear acrylic sealer. Diluted white glue will work, but colors tend to run more.

• 1" easel brushes for lettering and Mod-Poge

• ½" easel brushes for black lines (lead)

• Black poster paint

• Black electrical tape

The Butterfly Symbol

DIRECTIONS:

Using the pattern, cut a double thickness of tissue paper for wings. Attach rubber band to the middle of the antenna by twisting the chenille once. Fasten chenille around the head of the clothespin by twisting, and bend the tips so they look like antennas. Insert the wings into the clothespin slot and stretch the rubber band into the slot to hold the wings in place. Add eyes, mouth and other decorations if desired.

SUGGESTIONS FOR USE:

• Easter decorations for sanctuary, bulletin boards, classrooms, table decorations for Easter breakfast.

• Gifts for "shut-ins", convalescent homes, hospitals, congregation.

• They can be made into mobiles and hung from the ceiling.

MATERIALS:

• Colored tissue paper

• Butterfly wing pattern

• Scissors

• Clothespins (push type)

• Rubber bands

• 6" piece of chenille for antennas

• Felt pens

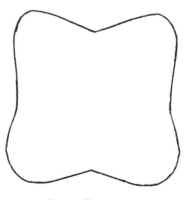

Butterfly pattern

The Egg Symbol

EGGS:

For thousands of years, even before the time of Jesus, the egg was used to symbolize new life. It was prominent in the spring festivals of many different cultures. Early Christians were quick to adopt the egg as a symbol of the resurrection and the new life that we find through Christ. The hard shell of the egg is a reminder of the stone that covered the tomb and was rolled away as Christ emerged triumphantly, conquering even death. The frail shell, like the tomb, is unable to hold the new life which is inside.

There are virtually thousands of things to do with eggs, and all of them can be used to enrich and reinforce the meaning of this favorite resurrection symbol. Check your local library for additional ideas.

PAPER EGGS:

Paper eggs can be cut from construction paper and decorated with crayon, felt pen, paint, collage, etc. Easter messages can be written on one side and the eggs hung from a thin dowel or tree branch. You can glue a toothpick to the bottom of the egg and fasten it inside a small nut cup size basket for a tray favor, table decoration, or gift.

PLASTIC EGGS:

Other resurrection symbols and messages can be placed inside the eggs and then given as gifts to the congregation, "shut-ins", convalescent homes, etc. The eggs can be decorated with permanent felt markers, tissue paper collage, or acrylic paint. Small sewing trims can also be glued to the eggs. Decorated eggs can be used in a church Easter egg hunt or given to children during Easter services.

PLASTER EGGS:

Egg ornaments can be made by pouring plaster of Paris into large serving spoons and inserting a paper clip or Christmas ornament hanger at the top. The dry egg forms are easy to paint and decorate using almost any method. Finished eggs make beautiful centerpieces when hung from small trees at an Easter breakfast.

STYROFOAM EGGS:

Sequins, trims, and beads can be fastened to the eggs with pins. If hollow styrofoam eggs are available, use small figures inside to tell the Easter story, like a peep box. Finished eggs can become part of a centerpiece, hung as a mobile, given as a gift to "shut-ins", or the congregation.

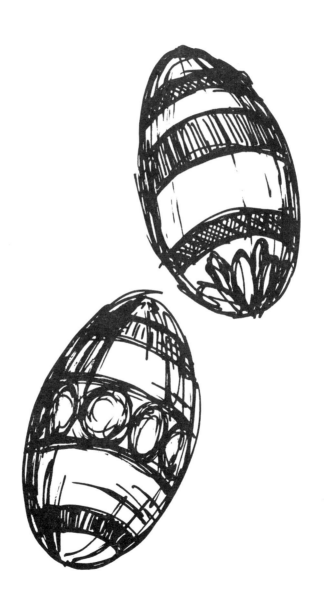

Christmas Bells

DIRECTIONS:

Make a hole in the bottom of clear plastic Communion cups with the small tip of a hot soldering iron. Dip the rims of each cup in white glue and then into glitter. When they are dry, string small metal bells inside with a fine wire which also serves as a hanger. A second bell, sprig of holly and a safety pin can change the bell from an ornament to a corsage.

SUGGESTIONS FOR USE:

• Give bells to the congregation as part of a Communion service during Advent.

• Use them as tray favors in hospitals.

• Give them as gifts when caroling.

MATERIALS:

• Plastic Communion cups

• Small soldering iron or similar tool to make a small hole in the bottom of each cup.

• Glitter, white glue

• Fine wire 4" lengths

• Saftey pins

• Small sprig of artificial holly or similar greenery

• Small round bells

FOOTNOTES

1. William Barclay, **The Gospel of Matthew, Vol. 1.,** pp. 215—219.

BIBLIOGRAPHY

Barclay, William. **The Gospel of Matthew Vol. 1.** Westminster Press, Philadelphia, 1975.

Daves, Michael. **Young Readers Book of Christian Symbolism.** Abington Press, New York, 1967.